UKULELE

CHART HITS
2022-2023
15 TOP HITS

ISBN 978-1-70518-863-7

For all works contained herein:
Unauthorized copying, arranging, adapting, recording, internet posting, public performance,
or other distribution of the music in this publication is an infringement of copyright.
Infringers are liable under the law.

Visit Hal Leonard Online at
www.halleonard.com

World headquarters, contact:
Hal Leonard
7777 West Bluemound Road
Milwaukee, WI 53213
Email: info@halleonard.com

In Europe, contact:
Hal Leonard Europe Limited
1 Red Place
London, W1K 6PL
Email: info@halleonardeurope.com

In Australia, contact:
Hal Leonard Australia Pty. Ltd.
4 Lentara Court
Cheltenham, Victoria, 3192 Australia
Email: info@halleonard.com.au

Anti-Hero

Words and Music by Taylor Swift and Jack Antonoff

* Vocal sung an octave lower than written.

Copyright © 2022 SONGS OF UNIVERSAL, INC., TASRM PUBLISHING, SONY MUSIC PUBLISHING (US) LLC and DUCKY DONATH MUSIC
All Rights for TASRM PUBLISHING Administered by SONGS OF UNIVERSAL, INC.
All Rights for SONY MUSIC PUBLISHING (US) LLC and DUCKY DONATH MUSIC Administered by
SONY MUSIC PUBLISHING (US) LLC, 424 Church Street, Suite 1200, Nashville, TN 37219
All Rights Reserved   Used by Permission

Pre-Chorus

should not be left to my own de - vic - es, they come with pric - es and
Did you hear my co - vert nar - cis - si - sm I dis - guise as al -

vic - es, I end up in cri - sis.
tru - is - m like some kind of con - gress - man?

I wake up scream - ing from dream - ing one day, I'll watch as you're leav -
I wake up scream - ing from dream - ing one day, I'll watch as you're leav -

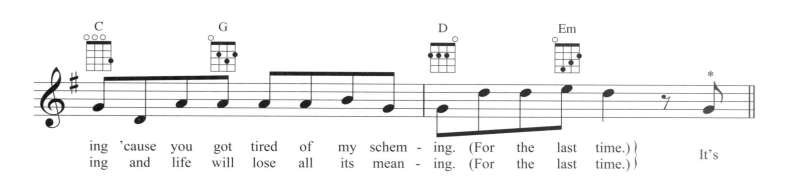

ing 'cause you got tired of my schem - ing. (For the last time.) It's
ing and life will lose all its mean - ing. (For the last time.)

Chorus 1

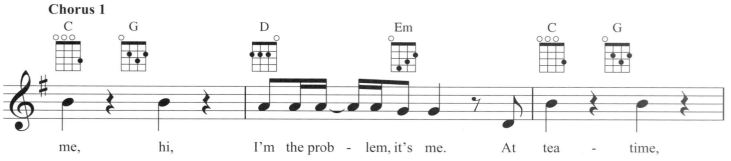

me, hi, I'm the prob - lem, it's me. At tea - time,

Vocal sung at pitch.

5

ev - 'ry-bod - y a - grees.   I'll stare di - rect - ly at the sun, ___

___ but nev - er in ___ the mir - ror. It ___ must be ex-haust - ing al - ways

root - ing for the an - ti - he - ro.   *(Instrumental)*

1.   **2.**   **Verse**

3. I have this dream, _ my daugh-ter - in -

- law kills me for ___ the mon - ey   she thinks I left ___ them in the will. _

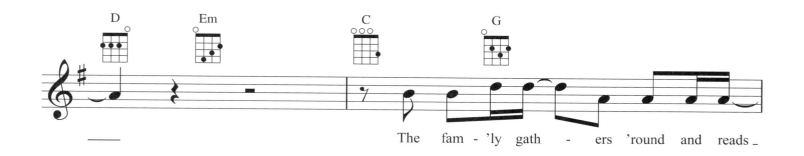

The fam - 'ly gath - ers 'round and reads _

_____ it and ___ then some - one screams _ out, "She's laugh-ing up ___ at us ___ from hell!" _

Chorus 2

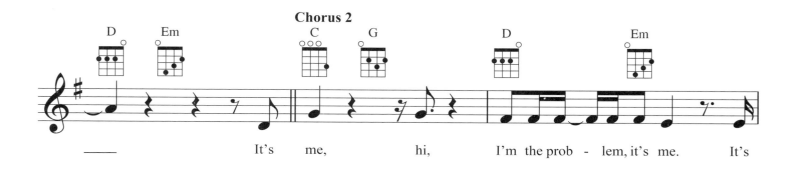

_____ It's me, hi, I'm the prob - lem, it's me. It's

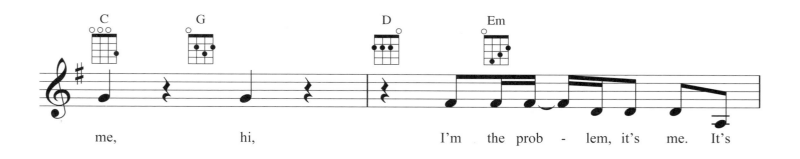

me, hi, I'm the prob - lem, it's me. It's

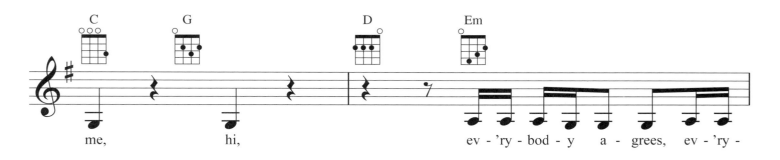

me, hi, ev - 'ry-bod - y a - grees, ev - 'ry -

bod - y   a - grees. _____   It's

Chorus 1

me,   hi,   I'm the prob - lem, it's me.   At tea -   time,

ev - 'ry - bod   -   y a - grees.   I'll stare di - rect - ly   at   the sun, _

____ but nev - er in ____ the mir - ror. It ____ must be ex - haust - ing al - ways

Outro

root - ing for the an - ti - he - ro.   *(Instrumental)*

Golden Hour

Words and Music by Jake Lawson and Zachary Lawson

First note

1. It was just two lov-ers sit-ting in the car

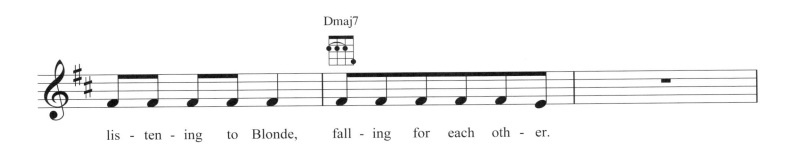

lis-ten-ing to Blonde, fall-ing for each oth-er.

Pink and orange skies, feel-ing su-per child-ish, no Don-ald Glov-er.

Missed call from my moth-er, like,

Copyright © 2022 Melodies By Seventy7 Music, Jvke Songz and Zvc Songz
All Rights Administered Worldwide by Kobalt Songs Music Publishing
All Rights Reserved   Used by Permission

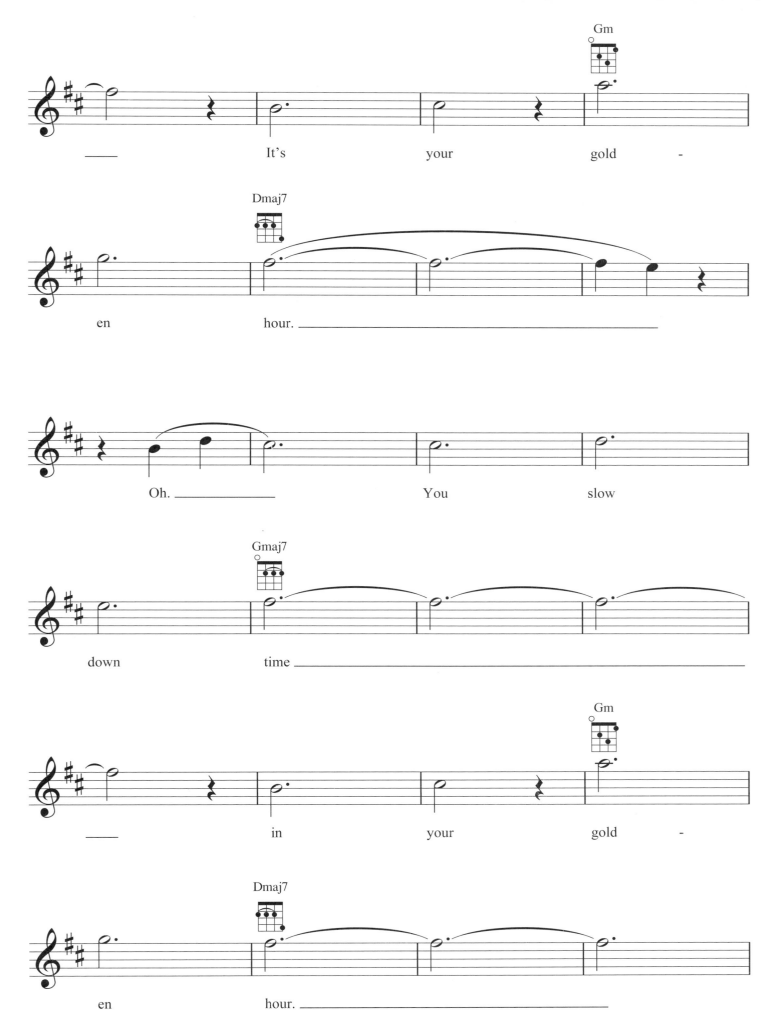

It's your gold -

en hour.

Oh. You slow

down time

in your gold -

en hour.

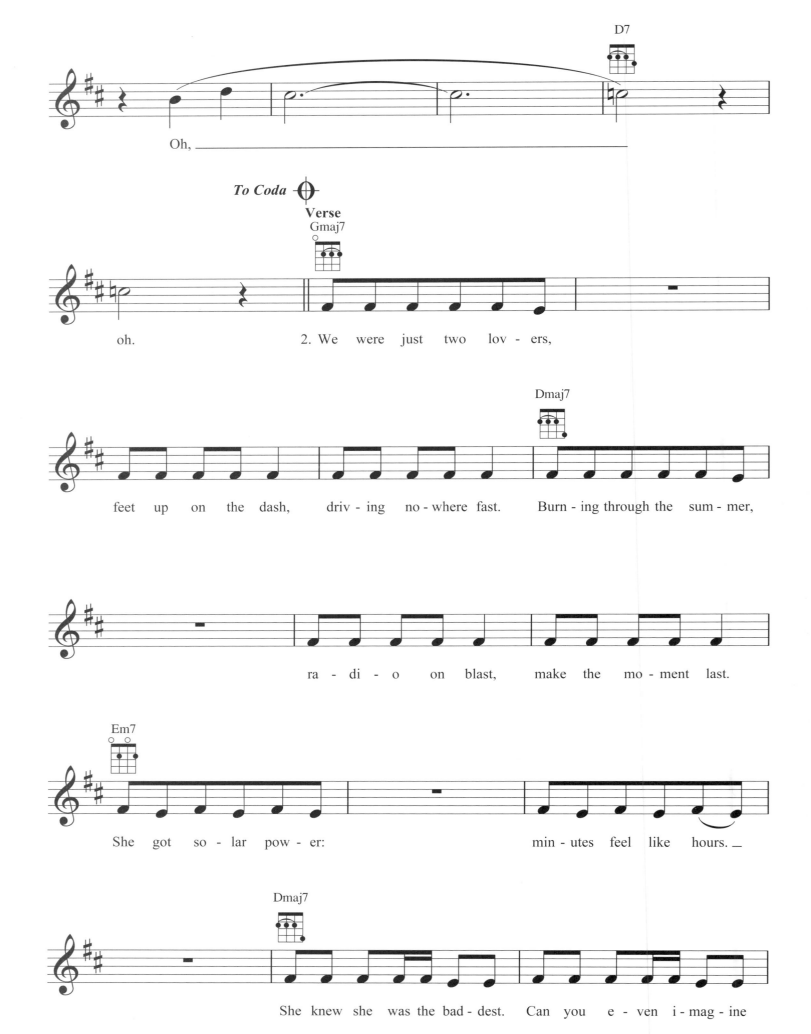

Oh, _____

To Coda ⊕

Verse

oh.   2. We were just two lov - ers,

feet up on the dash, driv - ing no - where fast.   Burn - ing through the sum - mer,

ra - di - o on blast,   make the mo - ment last.

She got so - lar pow - er: min - utes feel like hours. _

She knew she was the bad - dest. Can you e - ven i - mag - ine

Pre-Chorus

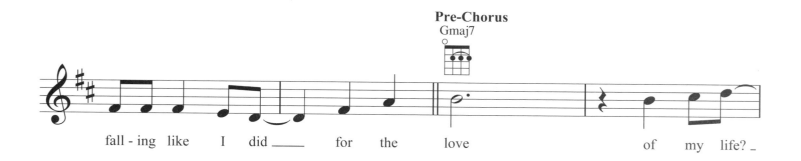

fall - ing like I did ____ for the love of my life? _

____ She's got glow on her face, a

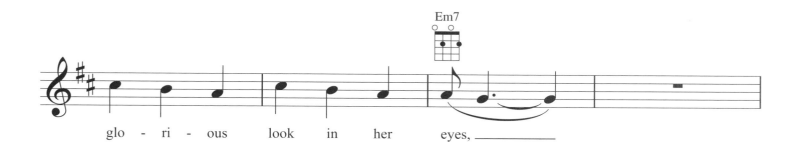

glo - ri - ous look in her eyes, _____

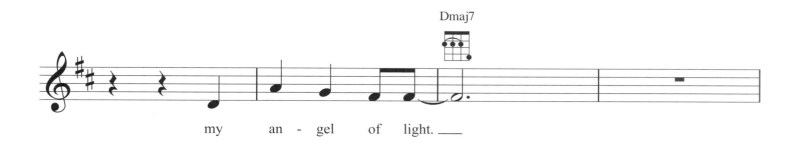

my an - gel of light. ____

D.S. al Coda

Coda

I was all a - lone ____ with the

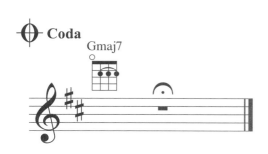

Celestial

Words and Music by Ed Sheeran, Johnny McDaid and Steve Mac

Copyright © 2022 Sony Music Publishing (UK) Limited, Sony Music Publishing (US) LLC and Rokstone Music
All Rights on behalf of Sony Music Publishing (UK) Limited and Sony Music Publishing (US) LLC
Administered by Sony Music Publishing(US) LLC, 424 Church Street, Suite 1200, Nashville, TN 37219
All Rights on behalf of Rokstone Music Administered by Universal-PolyGram International Publishing, Inc.
International Copyright Secured   All Rights Reserved

-ing out _____ in - to space. _____ Ce - les - ti - al. _____

Ce - les - ti - al. _____

1.

2.

Oh. _____

Bridge

We _____ were made to be

noth - ing more than this. Find - ing mag - ic in

all ___ the small - est ___ things. The way ___ we no - tice, that's

what real - ly mat - ters. ___ Let's make ___ to - night go

Bridge

on and on and on. ___ We ___ were made to be
You make me feel. _____

noth - ing more than this. Find - ing mag - ic in

all ___ the small - est ___ things. The way ___ we no - tice, that's
You make me feel. _____

what real - ly mat - ters. ___ Let's make ___ to - night go

Flowers

Words and Music by Miley Ray Cyrus, Gregory Hein and Michael Pollack

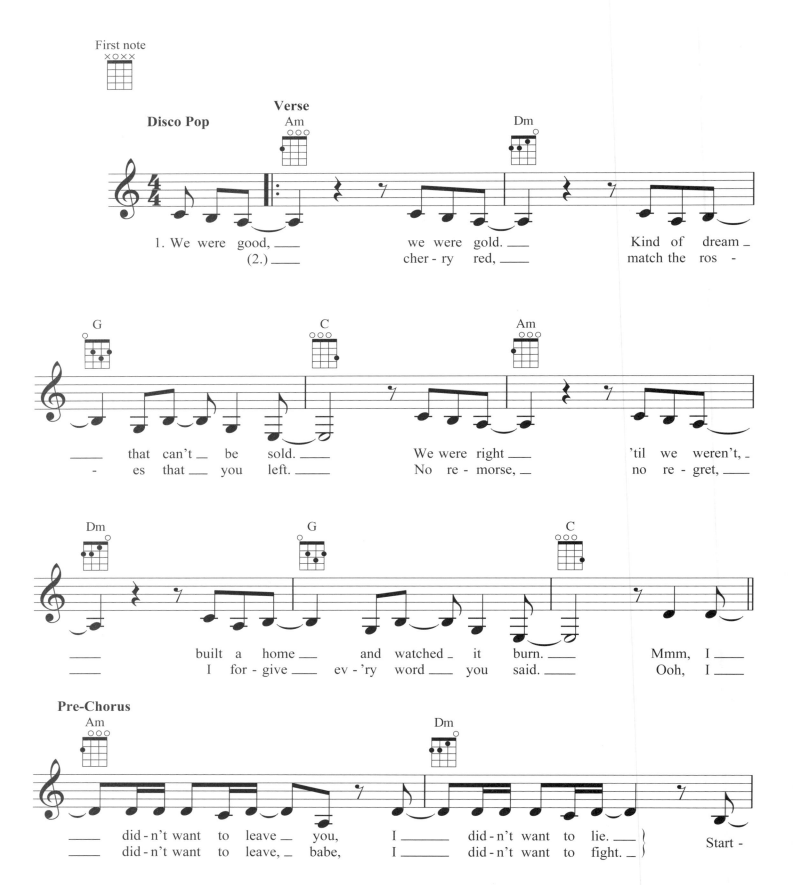

Copyright © 2023 Suga Bear Recordz Publishing, Concord Copyrights o/b/o These Are Pulse Songs, Songs By Gregory Hein,
Wide Eyed Global, Warner-Tamerlane Publishing Corp., Song With A Pure Tone and What Key Do You Want It In Music
All Rights on behalf of Suga Bear Recordz Publishing Administered by
Sony Music Publishing (US) LLC, 424 Church Street, Suite 1200, Nashville, TN 37219
All Rights on behalf of Concord Copyrights o/b/o These Are Pulse Songs, Songs By Gregory Hein
and Wide Eyed Global Administered by Concord Music Publishing
All Rights on behalf of Song With A Pure Tone and What Key Do You Want It In Music Administered by Warner-Tamerlane Publishing Corp.
International Copyright Secured   All Rights Reserved

- ed to cry, __ but then re - mem-bered I... __ I can buy my - self flow-

ers, write my name in the sand. __

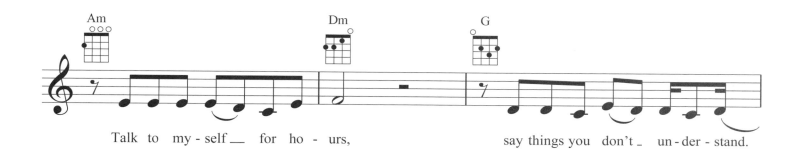

Talk to my - self __ for ho - urs, say things you don't __ un - der - stand.

__ I can take my - self danc - ing __

To Coda ⊕

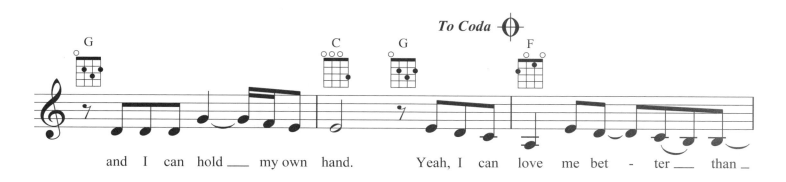

and I can hold __ my own hand. Yeah, I can love me bet - ter __ than __

you can. ____ (Can love me bet - ter,   I ____ can love me bet - ter, ba - by.

1.

Can love me bet - ter,   I ____ can love me bet - ter, ba - by.)
                                                      2. Paint my nails ___

2.

____ can love me bet - ter, ba - by.   Can love me bet - ter,   I ____ can love me bet - ter, ba - by.

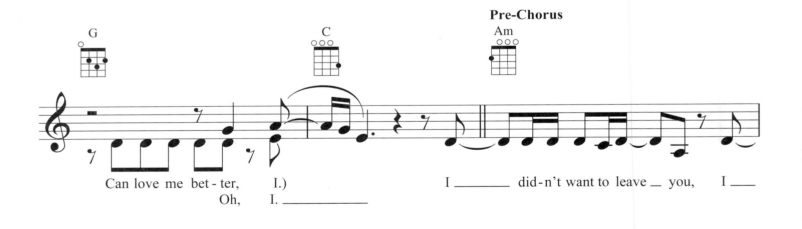

Pre-Chorus

Can love me bet - ter,   I.)   I ____ did - n't want to leave ___ you,   I ___
Oh,   I. _____

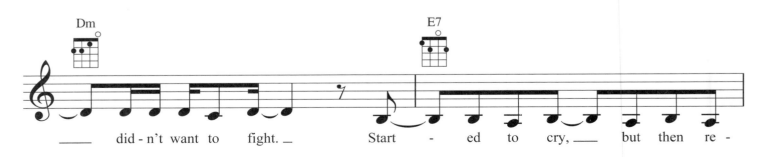

____ did - n't want to fight. __   Start - ed to cry, ___ but then re -

D.S. al Coda

mem-bered   I... ___

Coda

love   me   bet - ter ____ than, _

___   yeah, I can love   me bet - ter than ____   you ___ can. _

Outro

(Can love me bet-ter,   I _____ can love me bet-ter, ba-by.   Can love me bet-ter,   I ___

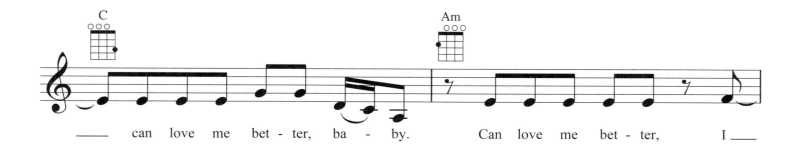

___   can love me bet - ter, ba - by.   Can love me bet - ter,   I ___

___   can love me bet - ter, ba - by.   Can love me bet - ter,   I.)

Forget Me

**Words and Music by Lewis Capaldi, Ben Kohn, Pete Kelleher,
Philip Plested, Tom Barnes and Michael Pollack**

Copyright © 2022 BMG Gold Songs, Sony Music Publishing (UK) Limited, Warner-Tamerlane Publishing Corp.,
What Key Do You Want It In Music and Songs With A Pure Tone
All Rights for BMG Gold Songs Administered by BMG Rights Management (US) LLC
All Rights for Sony Music Publishing (UK) Limited Administered by Sony Music Publishing (US) LLC, 424 Church Street, Suite 1200, Nashville, TN 37219
All Rights for What Key Do You Want It In Music and Songs With A Pure Tone Administered by Warner-Tamerlane Publishing Corp.
All Rights Reserved   Used by Permission

and you're not wrong. _____ Well,

I'll take all the vit - ri - ol, but not the thought of you mov - ing on. _

Chorus

'Cause I'm _ not read - y to

find out you know how to for - get ____ me. I'd

rath - er hear how much you re - gret ____ me and

pray to God that you nev - er met ____ me, than for - get ____ me. Oh, _ I _____

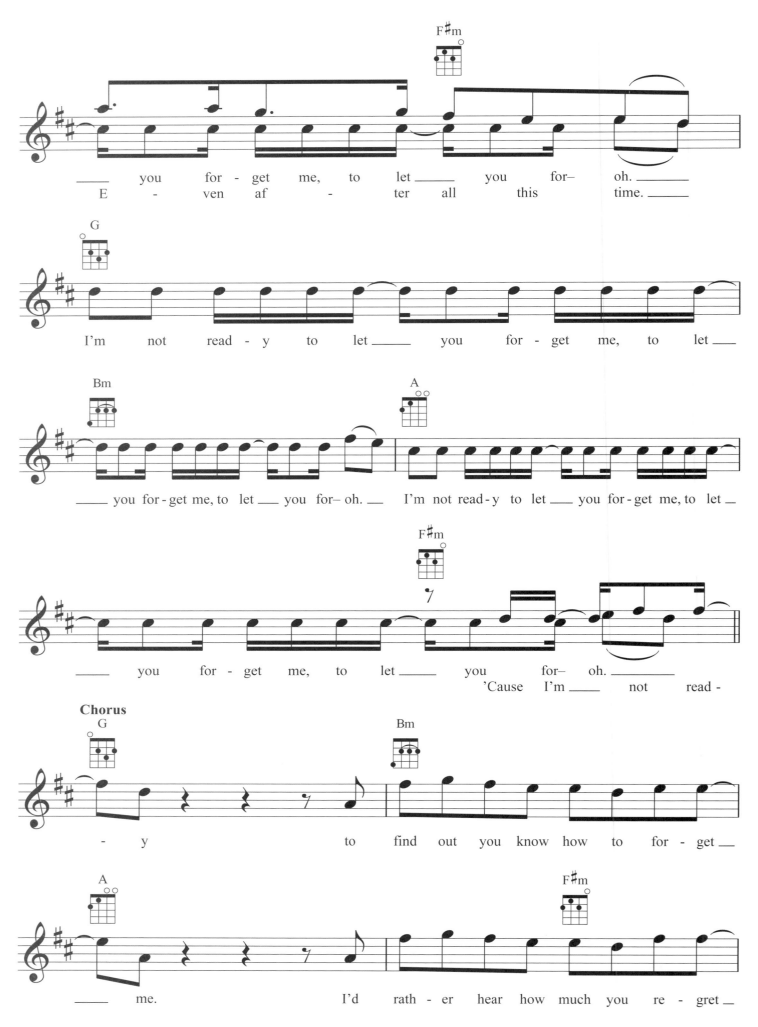

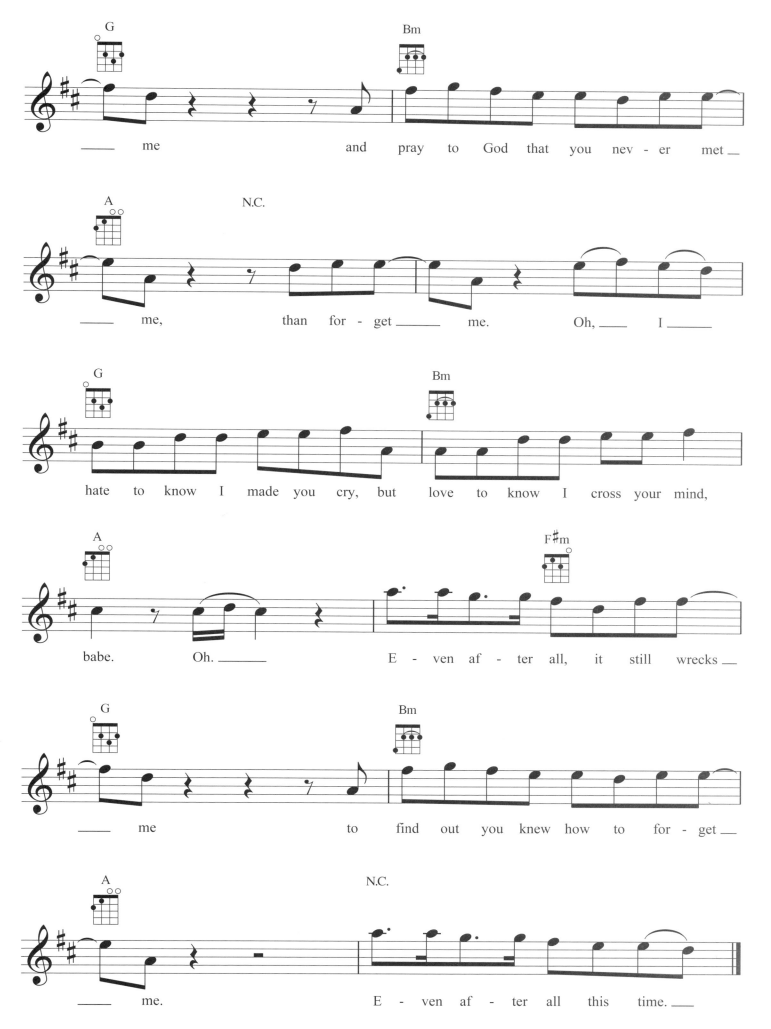

Left and Right

Words and Music by Charlie Puth and Jacob Kasher Hindlin

First note

Intro-Chorus
Moderate Pop

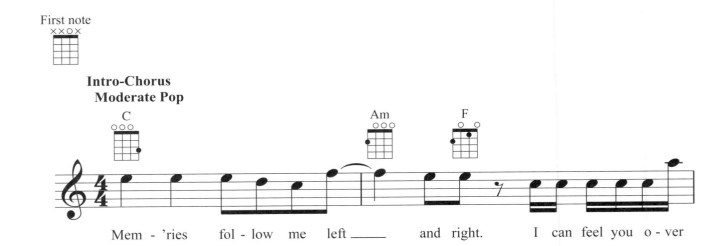

Mem - 'ries fol - low me left _____ and right. I can feel you o - ver

here, I can feel you o - ver here. You take up ev - 'ry cor - ner of my mind. 1. What you gon' do

Verse

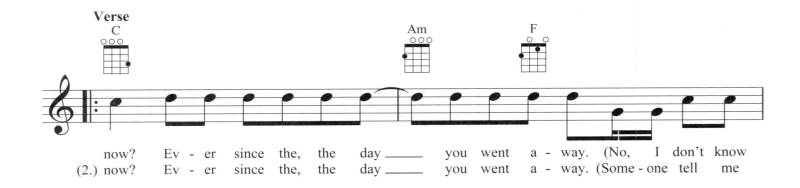

now? Ev - er since the, the day _____ you went a - way. (No, I don't know
(2.) now? Ev - er since the, the day _____ you went a - way. (Some - one tell me

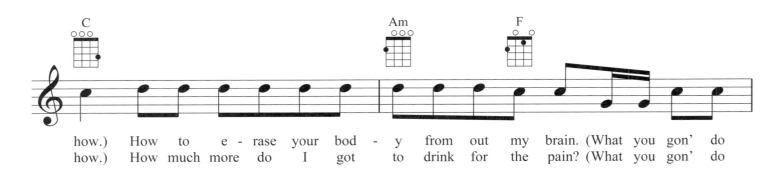

how.) How to e - rase your bod - y from out my brain. (What you gon' do
how.) How much more do I got to drink for the pain? (What you gon' do

Copyright © 2022 Charlie Puth Music Publishing, Artist 101 Publishing Group, Prescription Songs and Kobalt Music Services America, Inc
All Rights for Charlie Puth Music Publishing and Artist 101 Publishing Group Administered Worldwide by Songs Of Kobalt Music Publishing
All Rights for Prescription Songs Administered Worldwide by Kobalt Songs Music Publishing
All Rights Reserved   Used by Permission

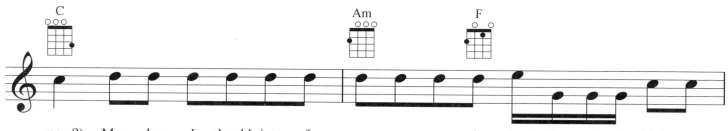

now?) May - be I should just fo - cus on me in - stead. (But all I think a -
now?) You do things to me that I just can't for - get. (Now all I think a -

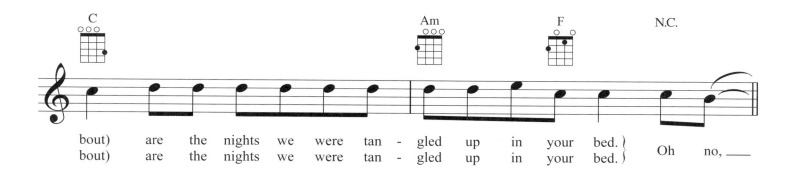

bout) are the nights we were tan - gled up in your bed. }
bout) are the nights we were tan - gled up in your bed. } Oh no, ___

Pre-Chorus

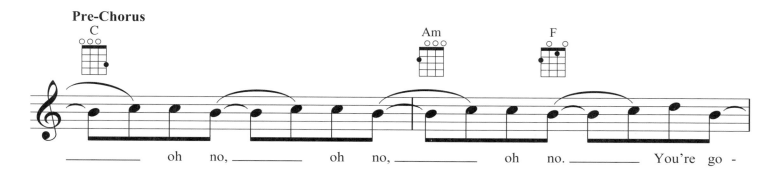

___ oh no, ___ oh no, ___ oh no. ___ You're go -

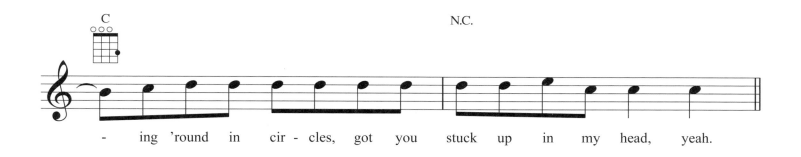

- ing 'round in cir - cles, got you stuck up in my head, yeah.

Chorus

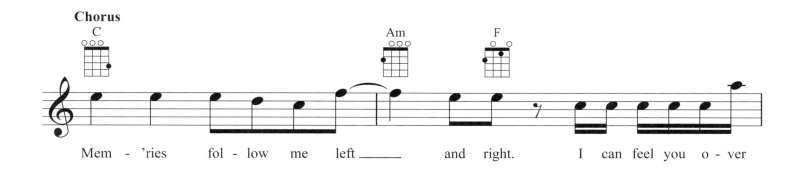

Mem - 'ries fol - low me left ___ and right. I can feel you o - ver

here, I can feel you o - ver here. You take up ev -'ry cor - ner of my mind.

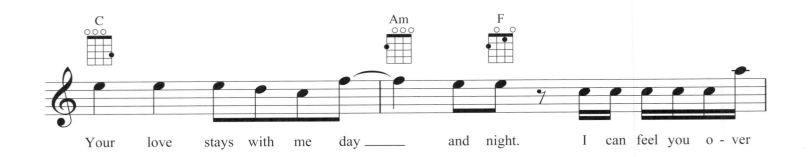
Your love stays with me day _____ and night. I can feel you o - ver

here, I can feel you o - ver here. You take up ev - 'ry

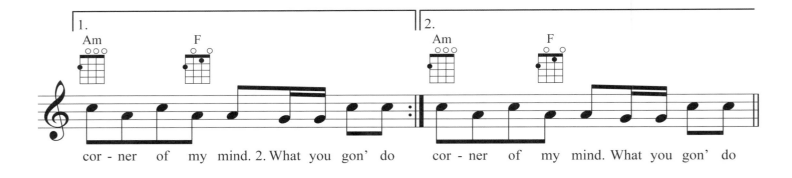
1.
cor - ner of my mind. 2. What you gon' do
2.
cor - ner of my mind. What you gon' do

Bridge
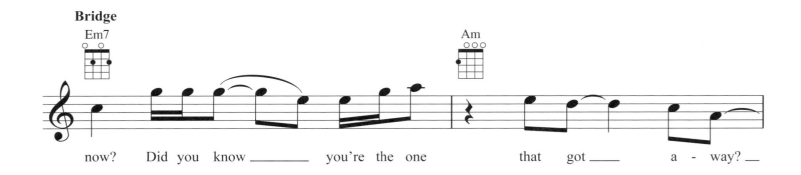
now? Did you know _____ you're the one that got _____ a - way? __

And e-ven now, _____ ba-by, I'm still not _____ o-kay. __

__ Did you know _____ that my dreams, __ they're all _____ the same? __

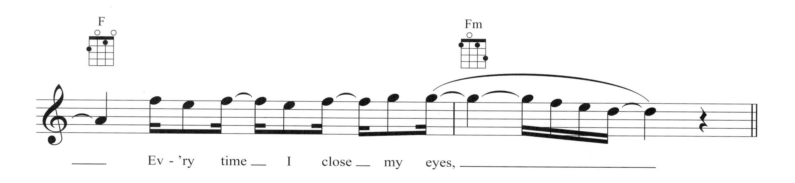

__ Ev-'ry time __ I close __ my eyes, _____

Chorus

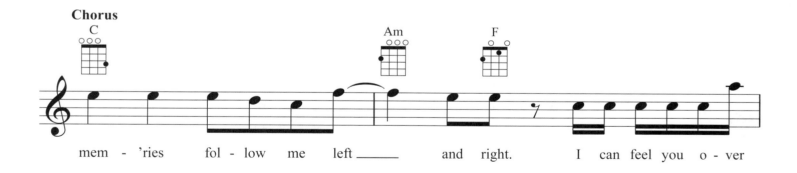

mem-'ries fol-low me left _____ and right. I can feel you o-ver

here, I can feel you o-ver here. You take up ev-'ry

cor - ner of my mind. Your love stays with me day __
(What you gon' do now?)

__ and night. I can feel you o - ver here, I can feel you o - ver here. You take up ev -'ry

Outro

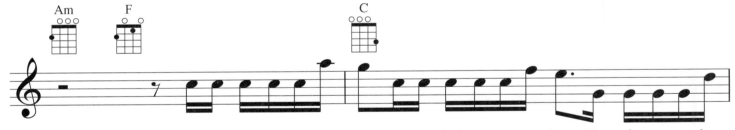

cor - ner of my mind. What you gon' do now?

I can feel you o - ver here, I can feel you o - ver here. You take up ev -'ry

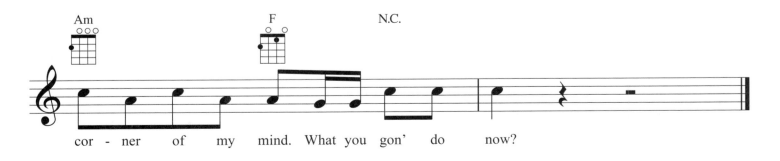

cor - ner of my mind. What you gon' do now?

I Ain't Worried

from TOP GUN: MAVERICK

**Words and Music by Ryan Tedder, Brent Kutzle, Tyler Spry,
Björn Yttling, John Eriksson and Peter Moren**

Copyright © 2022 Singles Only Please, Acornman Music, Foxodega, One Stop Pop Shop and EMI Music Publishing Scandinavia AB
All Rights for Singles Only Please, Acornman Music, Foxodega Tend One Stop Pop Shop Administered by Downtown Music Services
All Rights for EMI Music Publishing Scandinavia AB Administered by Sony Music Publishing (US) LLC,
424 Church Street, Suite 1200, Nashville, TN 37219
All Rights Reserved   Used by Permission

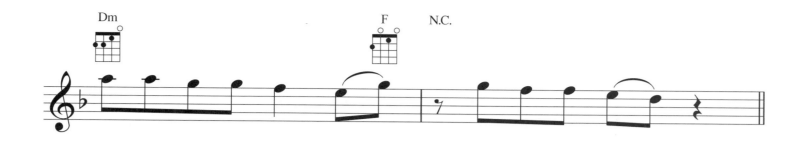

Verse

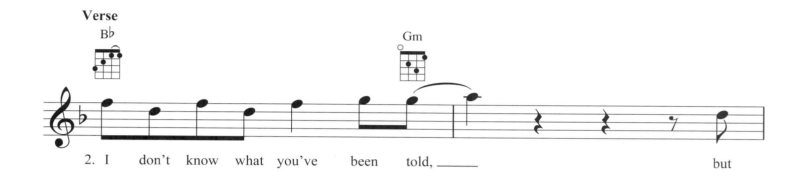

2. I   don't   know   what   you've   been   told, _____   but

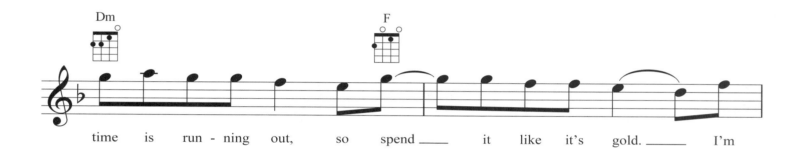

time   is   run - ning   out,   so   spend ____   it   like   it's   gold. _____   I'm

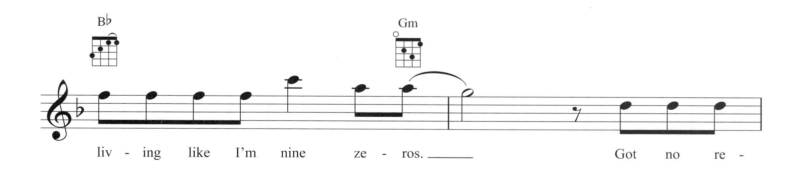

liv - ing   like   I'm   nine   ze - ros. _____   Got   no   re -

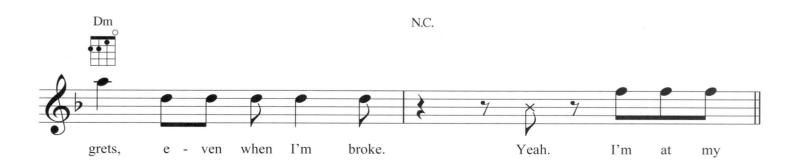

grets,   e - ven   when   I'm   broke.   Yeah.   I'm   at   my

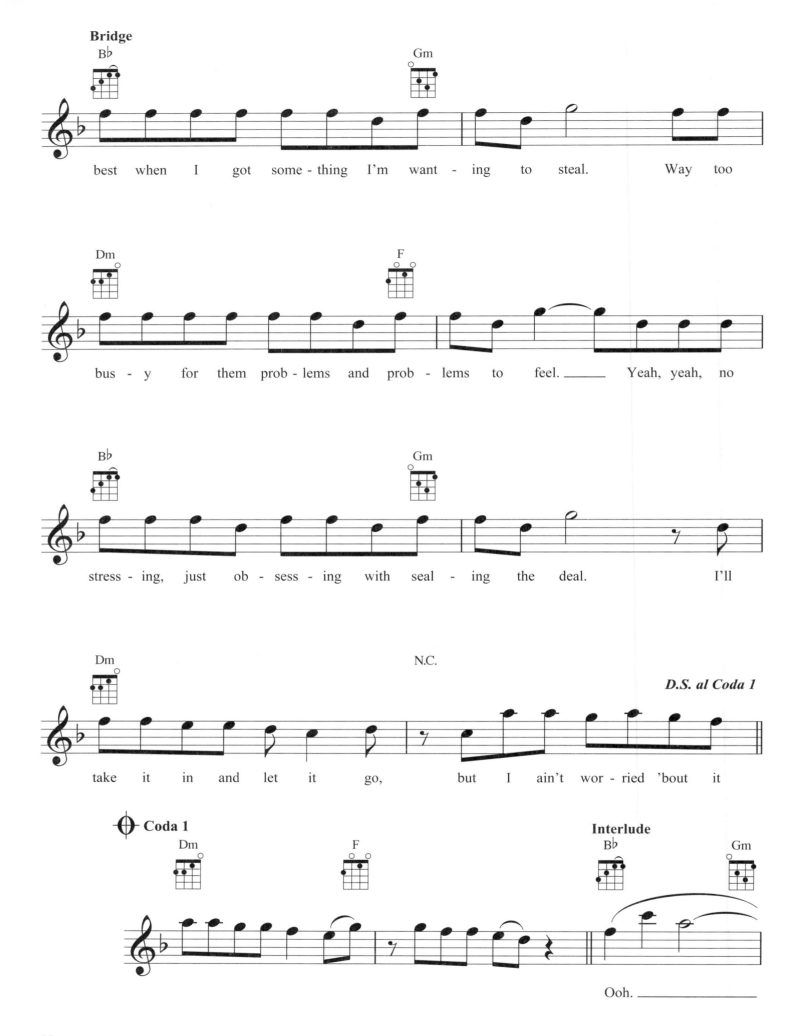

I

ain't ___ wor - ried. _____ Ooh. _____

Oh, _____ no. ___

D.S. al Coda 2

N.C.

___ I ain't wor - ried 'bout it

⊕ Coda 2

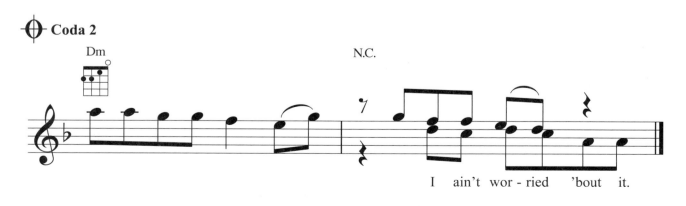

I ain't wor - ried 'bout it.

Lift Me Up

from BLACK PANTHER: WAKANDA FOREVER

Words and Music by Robyn Fenty, Temilade Openiyi, Ludwig Göransson and Ryan Coogler

Copyright © 2022 Monica Fenty Music Publishing, Sony Music Publishing (UK) Ltd., Ludovin Music and Marvel Superheroes Music
All Rights on behalf of Monica Fenty Music Temibling and Sony Music Publishing (UK) Ltd. Administered by
Sony Music Publishing (US) LLC, 424 Church Street, Suite 1200, Nashville, TN 37219
All Rights on behalf of Ludovin Music Administered by Songs Of Universal, Inc.
International Copyright Secured   All Rights Reserved

Verse

1. Burn - ing ___ in a hope - less dream, ___
2. Drown - ing ___ in an end - less sea, ___

hold me ___ when you go to sleep. ___
take some _ time and stay with me. ___

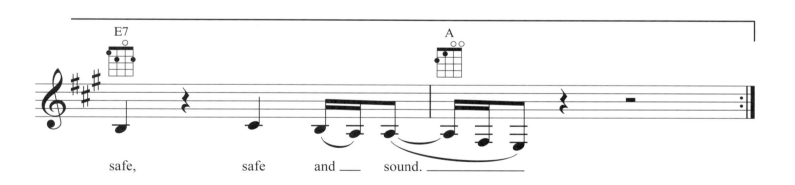

Keep ___ me in the warmth of your love. When you de - part, ___ keep me
Keep ___ me in the strength of your

safe, safe and ___ sound. ___

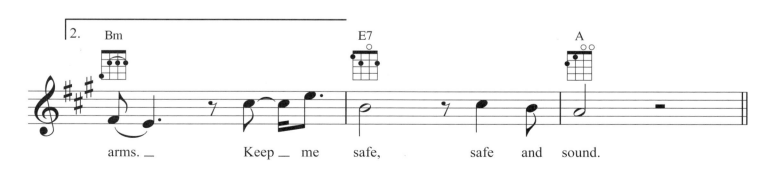

arms. ___ Keep _ me safe, safe and sound.

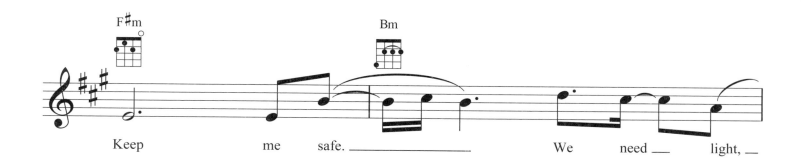

Keep   me safe. _____ We need ___ light, ___

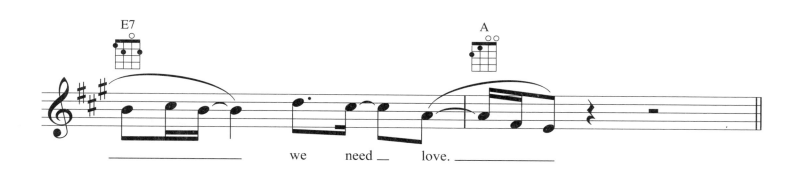

_____ we need __ love. _____

Chorus

Lift ____ me up   in _____ your arms. _____

Lift   me   up,

I ____ need love, I ____ need love, I ___ need __ love. _____

hold   me   down.

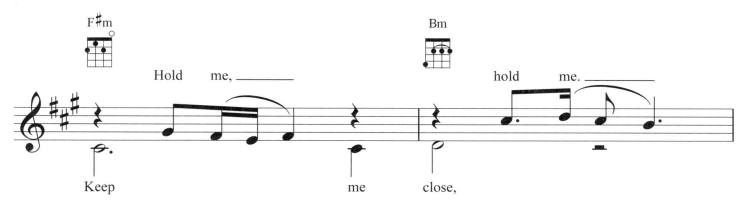

Hold me, _____   hold me. _____

Keep   me close,

Quietly Yours

featured in the Netflix film PERSUASION
Words and Music by Jasmine Van Den Bogaerde

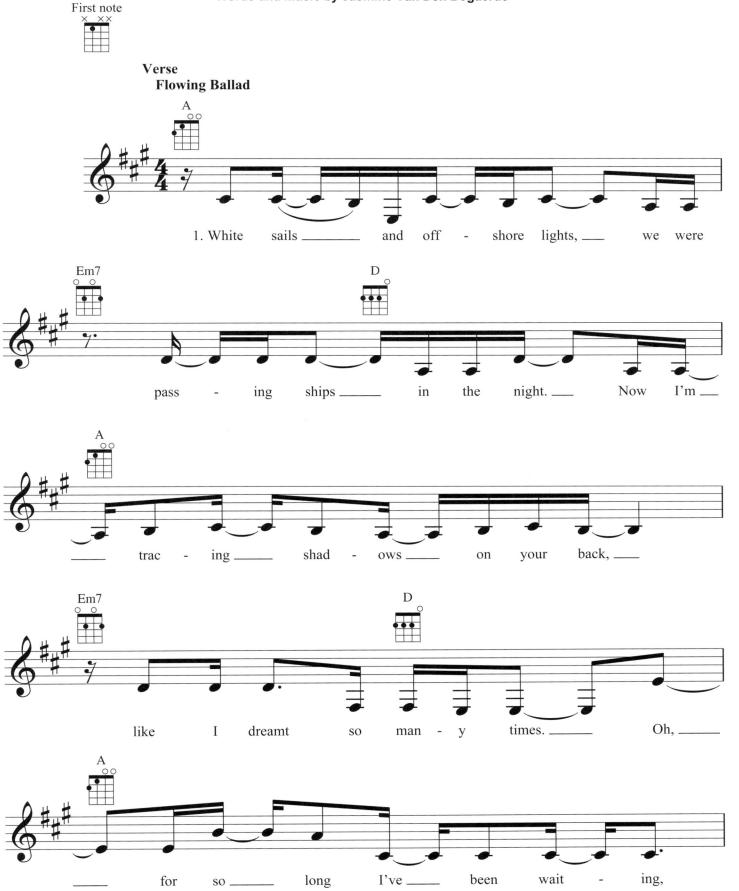

Copyright © 2022 Maisie Anthems and Maisie Beats
Rights Administered by BMG Rights Management (US) LLC
All Rights Reserved   Used by Permission

for so _____ long for a love like this. _____ And I _____

_____ was so sure, ba - by, I'd lost _____ you for a min - ute, but...

𝄋 Chorus

There's the sweet - est _____

spring at my door. ___ Can you feel _____ it? Just the

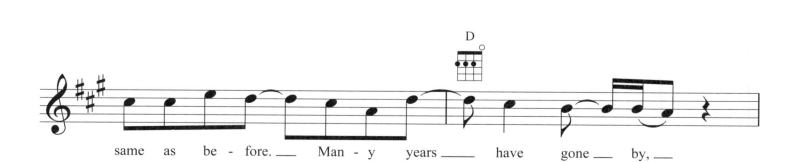

same as be - fore. ___ Man - y years _____ have gone ___ by, ___

but I knew you'd come. ___   Qui - et - ly keep -

- ing   this hope in my heart. Prayed the night ___ bring

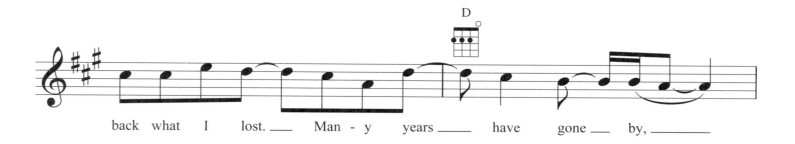

back what I lost. ___ Man - y years ___ have gone ___ by, _____

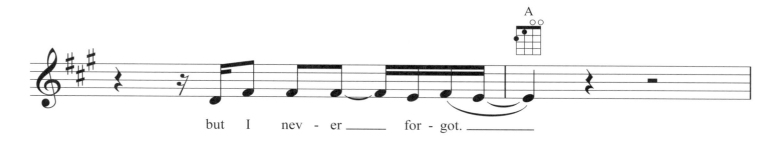

but I nev - er _____ for - got. _____

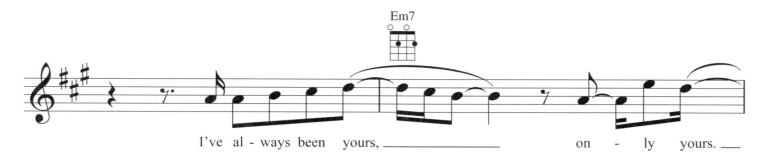

I've al - ways been yours, _____ on - ly yours. ___

_____   Mm. ___

To Coda

Verse

2. There was a time when I ____ let you go,

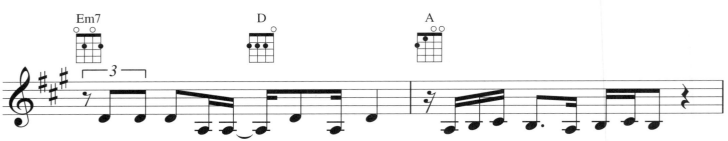

'lowed my-self to be ____ swayed and pulled. For all my days I make a vow,

no words ____ could ev-er shake me now. 'Cause ____ for so ____ long I've ____ been wait-ing,

for so ____ long for a love like this. ____ And I _____ was so sure, ba-by, I'd lost ____

D.S. al Coda

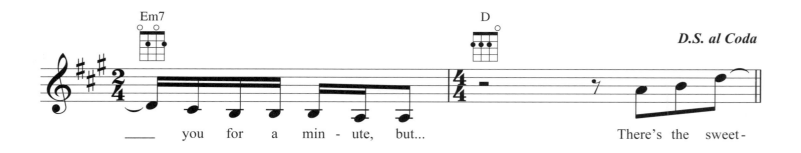

____ you for a min-ute, but... There's the sweet-

48

Nothing Is Lost

(You Give Me Strength)

from AVATAR: THE WAY OF WATER
Words by Abel Tesfaye
Music by Abel Tesfaye, Steve Angello, Sebastian Ingrosso, Axel Hedfors and Simon Franglen

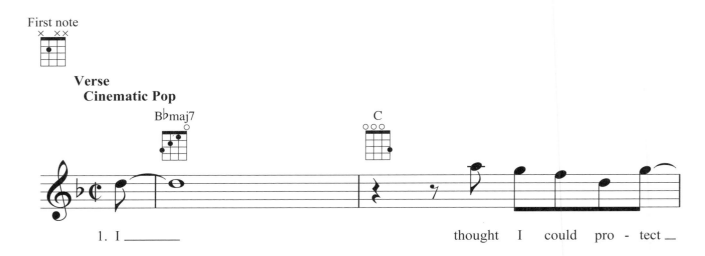

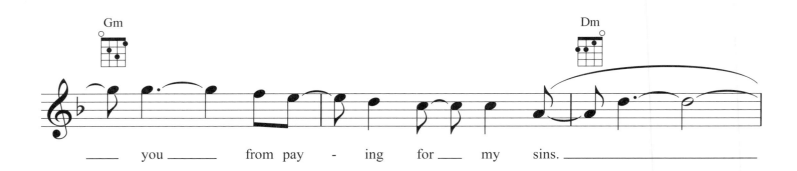

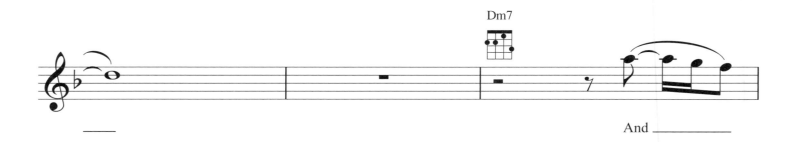

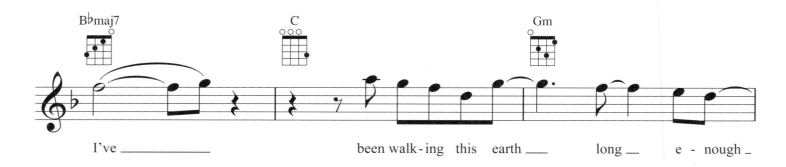

Copyright © 2022 XO Music Publishing LLC, Sebastian Ingrosso Publishing Designee, Axel Hedfors Publishing Designee,
Fairwood Music, Twentieth Screen Music, Inc., Fox Film Music Corp. and T C F Music Publishing, Inc.
All Rights Reserved   Used by Permission

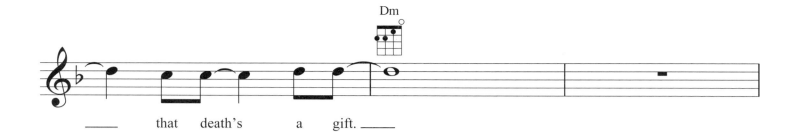

that death's a gift. ____

𝄋 **Pre-Chorus**

Been liv - ing this life ___ so pa - tient _____

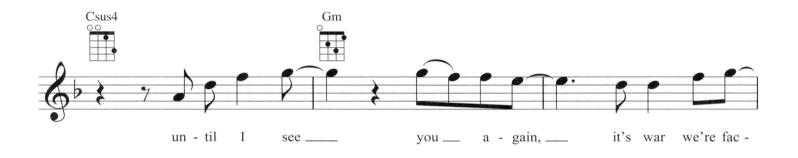

un - til I see ____ you __ a - gain, ___ it's war we're fac -

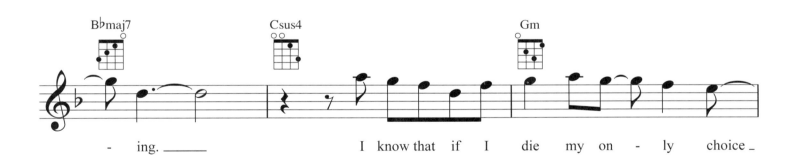

- ing. _____ I know that if I die my on - ly choice _

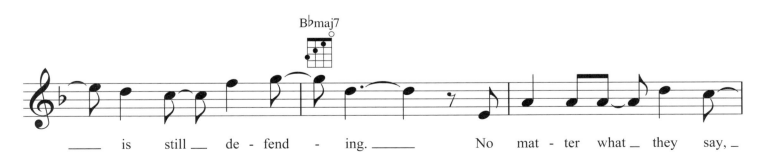

____ is still __ de - fend - ing. _____ No mat - ter what __ they say, _

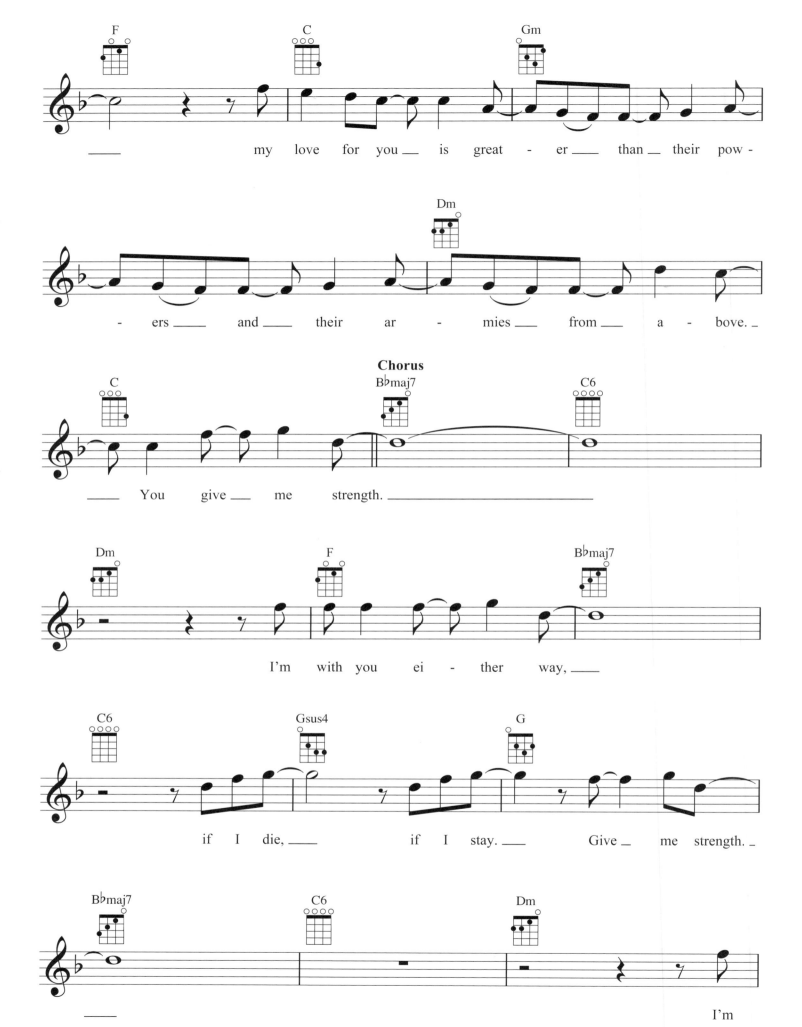

my love for you ___ is great - er ___ than ___ their pow -

- ers ___ and ___ their ar - mies ___ from ___ a - bove. ___

Chorus

___ You give ___ me strength. ___

I'm with you ei - ther way, ___

if I die, ___ if I stay. ___ Give ___ me strength. ___

I'm

with you   ei - ther   way. _____   Noth-ing's lost, __

To Coda ⊕

Interlude

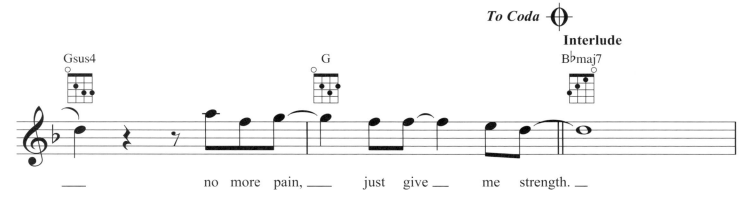

__   no more   pain, __   just   give __   me   strength. __

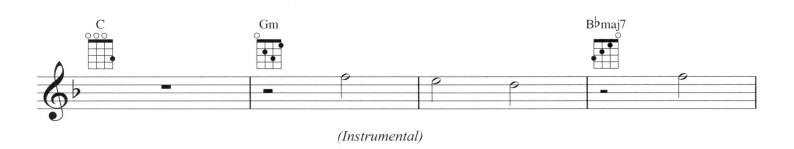

(Instrumental)

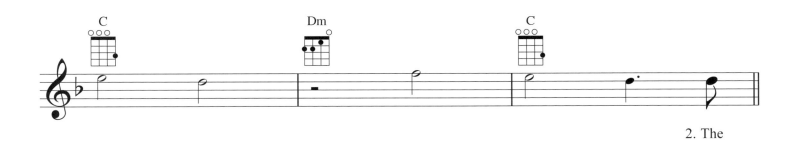

2. The

Verse

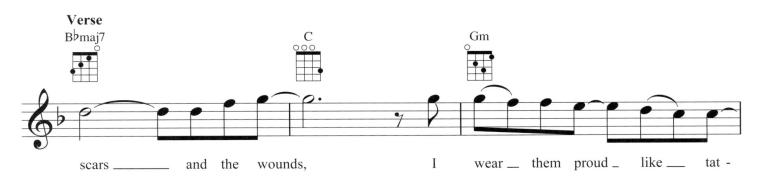

scars _____ and   the   wounds,   I   wear __ them   proud __ like __   tat -

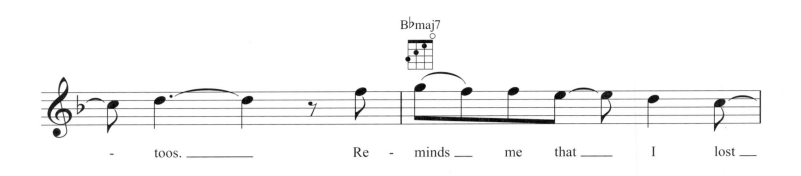

- toos. _____ Re - minds ___ me that ____ I lost ___

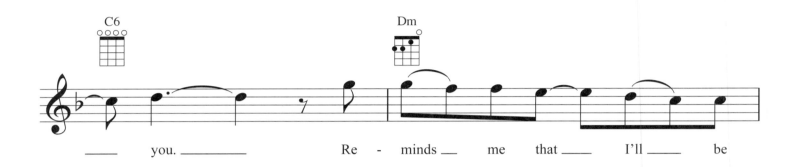

_____ you. _____ Re - minds ___ me that ____ I'll ____ be

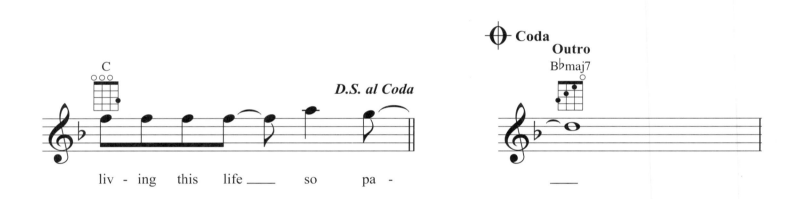

liv - ing this life ____ so pa - ____

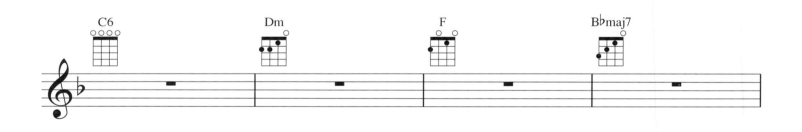

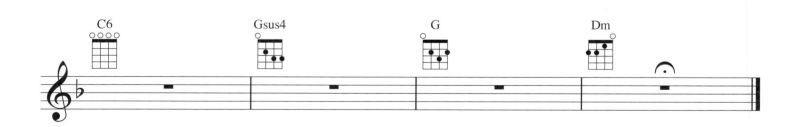

Sunroof

Words and Music by Nicholas Minutaglio, Nicholas Ure and Aidan Rodriguez

First note

Intro
Up-tempo Pop

La da la da da ___ la da da. ___ La da la da di da

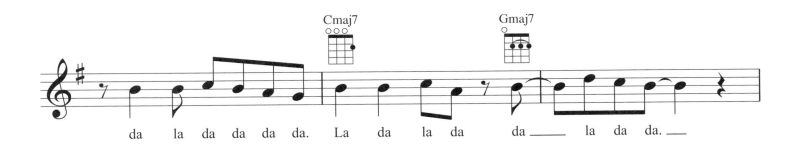

da la da da da da. La da la da da ___ la da da. ___

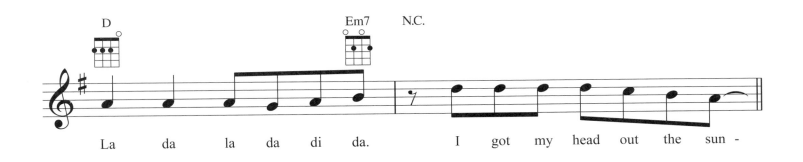

La da la da di da. I got my head out the sun-

Chorus

-roof, I'm blast-ing our fa-v'rite tunes. I on-ly got one ___

Copyright © 2021, 2022 Sony Music Publishing (US) LLC, Dazy Music,
Songs Of Universal, Inc., Nicky Youre Music and Aidan Rodriguez Publishing Designee
All Rights on behalf of Sony Music Publishing (US) LLC and Dazy Music Administered by
Sony Music Publishing (US) LLC, 424 Church Street, Suite 1200, Nashville, TN 37219
All Rights on behalf of Nicky Youre Music Administered by Songs Of Universal, Inc.
International Copyright Secured   All Rights Reserved

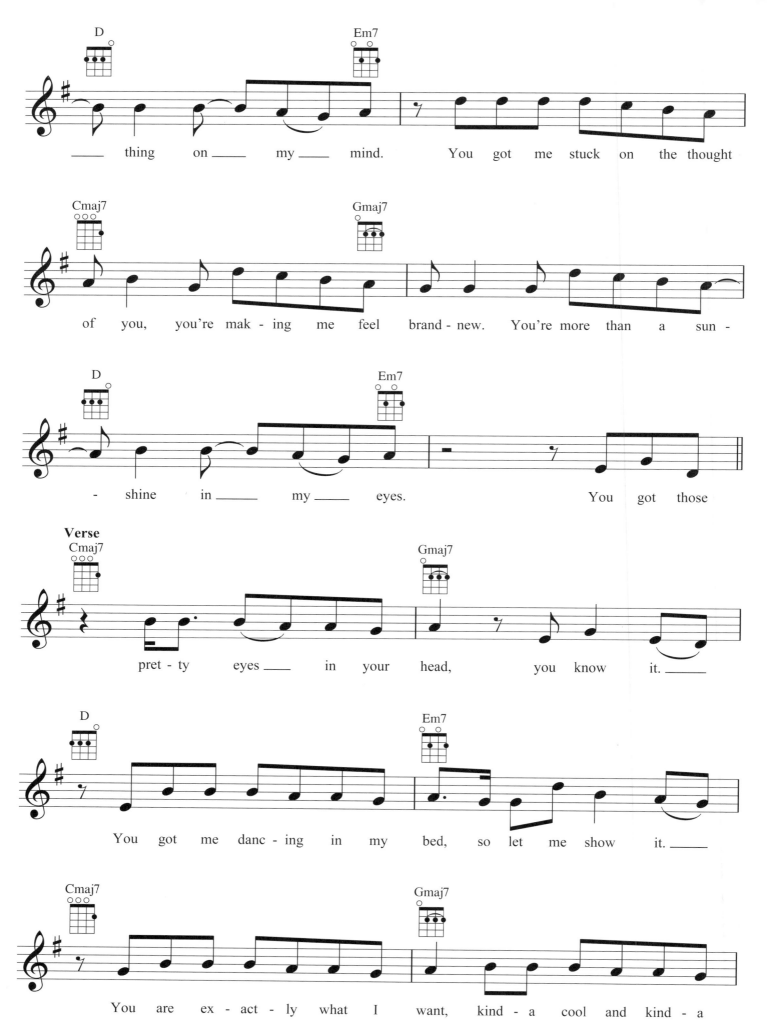

thing on ___ my ___ mind. You got me stuck on the thought

of you, you're mak - ing me feel brand - new. You're more than a sun -

- shine in ___ my ___ eyes. You got those

Verse

pret - ty eyes ___ in your head, you know it. ___

You got me danc - ing in my bed, so let me show it. ___

You are ex - act - ly what I want, kind - a cool and kind - a

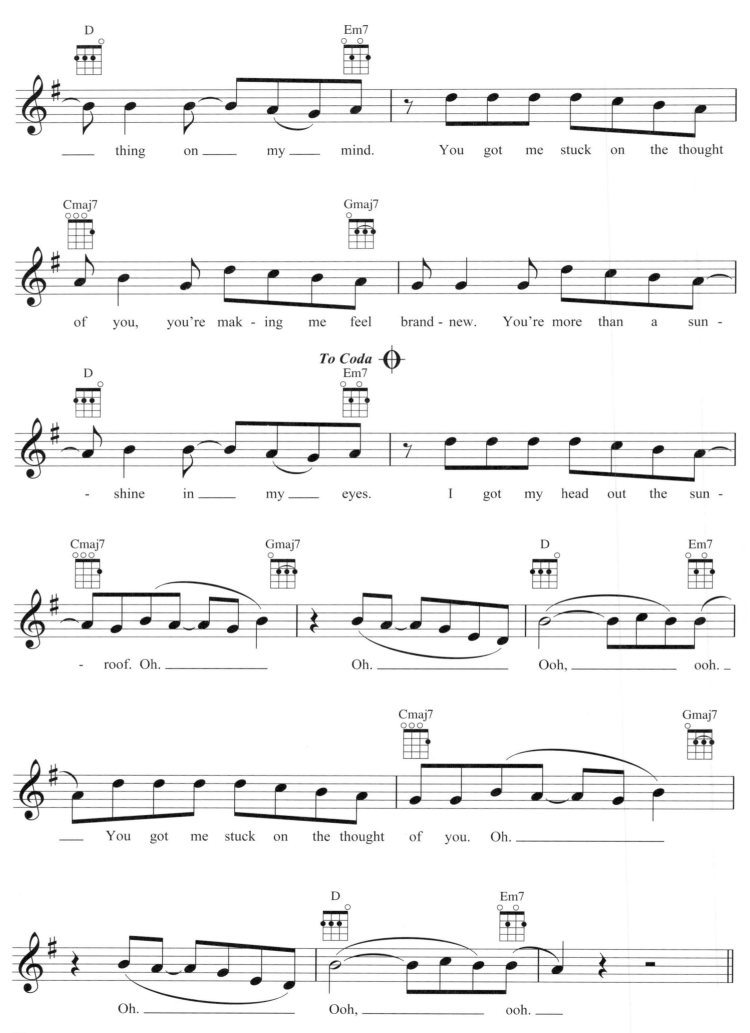

58

Interlude

(Instrumental)

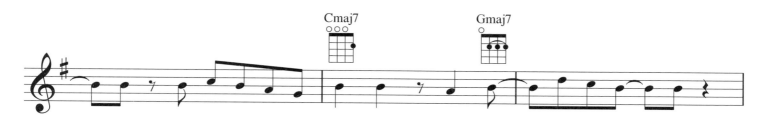

Yeah, __ we're

Outro

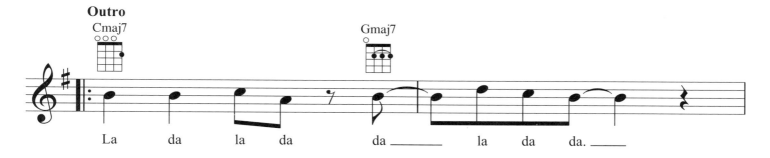

La   da   la   da   da _____   la   da   da. _____

La   da   la   da   di   da   da   la   da   da   da   da.   La   da   la   da   da __

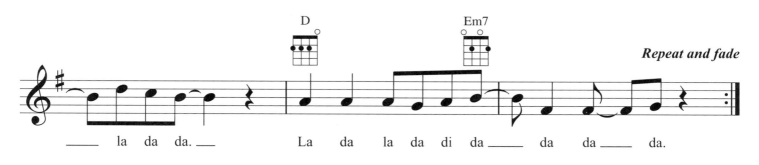

_____   la   da   da. __   La   da   la   da   di   da _____   da   da _____   da.

Something in the Orange

Words and Music by Zachary Lane Bryan

© 2022 WARNER-TAMERLANE PUBLISHING CORP. and ZACHARY BRYAN BMI PUB DESIGNEE
All Rights Administered by WARNER-TAMERLANE PUBLISHING CORP.
All Rights Reserved   Used by Permission

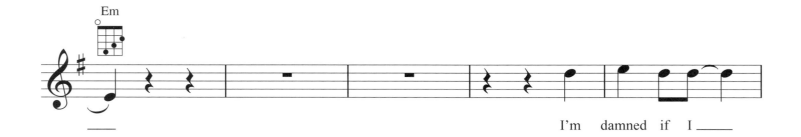

I'm damned if I ____

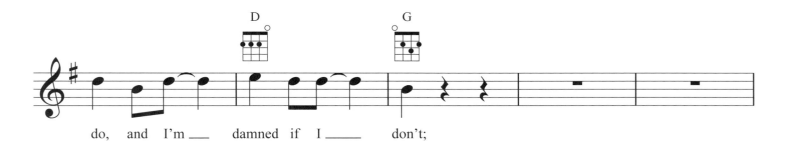

do, and I'm ___ damned if I ____ don't;

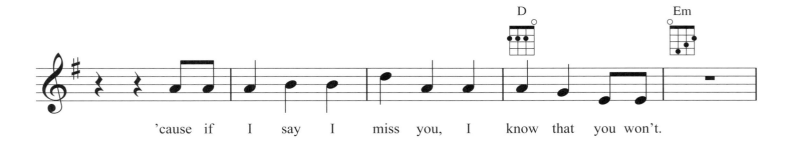

'cause if I say I miss you, I know that you won't.

But I miss you in the morn - ings when I ___

____ see the sun. ___

Some - thing in the or - ange tells me we're not ___ done.

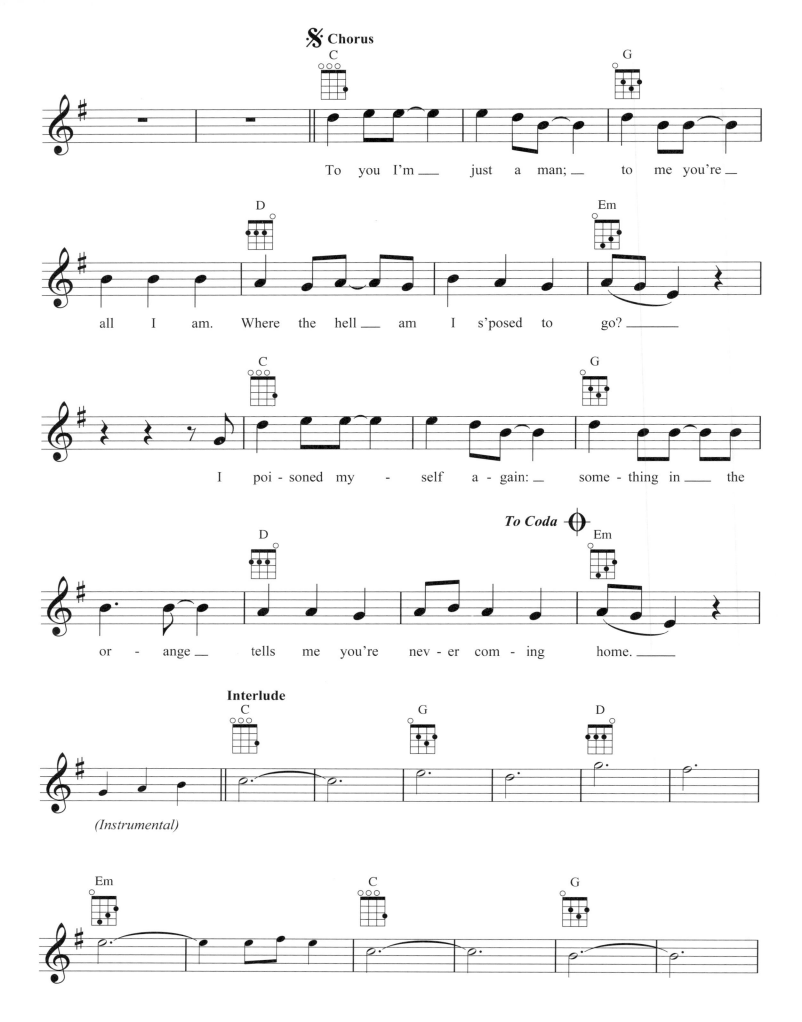

Verse

2. Need to hear you

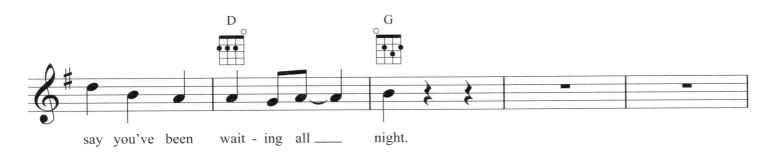

say you've been wait - ing all ____ night.

There's or - ange danc - ing in your eyes ___ from bulb ___ light.

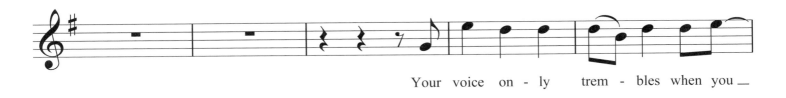

Your voice on - ly trem - bles when you ___

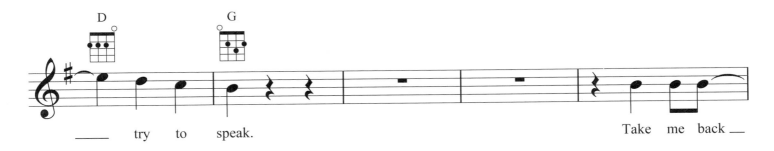

____ try to speak. Take me back ___

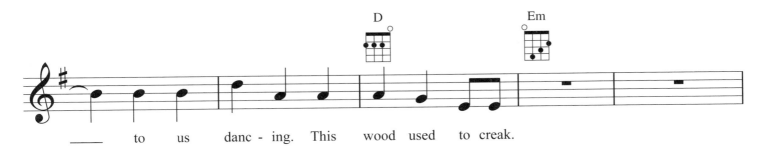

____ to us danc - ing. This wood used to creak.

D.S. al Coda

Coda

Interlude

home. ___

(Instrumental)

Chorus

To   you   I'm ___   just   a   man; ___

to   me   you're ___   all   I   am.   Where   the   hell ___   am   I   s'posed   to

go? _____

I   poi - soned   my - self   a - gain: ___

Outro

some - thing in ___ the or - ange ___ tells me you're nev - er com - ing

home. ___ If you leave to - day, ___ I'll just

stare at the way ___ the or - ange touch - es all things a - round. ___

___ The grass, trees, and dew, how ___

I just hate ___ you. Please turn those head - lights a - round. ___

Please turn those head - lights a - round. ___

TV

Words and Music by Billie Eilish O'Connell and Finneas O'Connell

Copyright © 2022 UNIVERSAL MUSIC CORP., DRUP and LAST FRONTIER
All Rights for DRUP Administered by UNIVERSAL MUSIC CORP.
All Rights for LAST FRONTIER Administered Worldwide by KOBALT SONGS MUSIC PUBLISHING
All Rights Reserved   Used by Permission

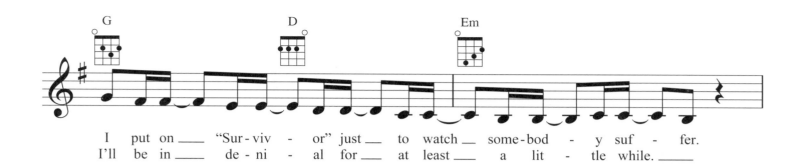

I put on _____ "Sur - viv - or" just _____ to watch _____ some - bod - y suf - fer.
I'll be in _____ de - ni - al for _____ at least _____ a lit - tle while. _____

May - be I should get some _____ sleep. _____
What a - bout the plans we _____ made? _____ The

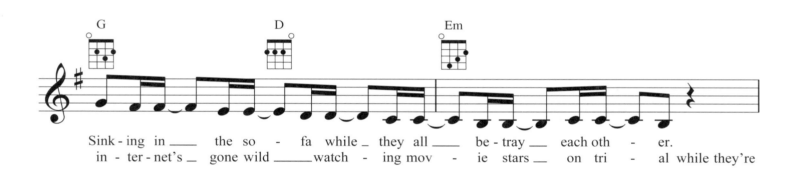

Sink - ing in _____ the so - fa while _____ they all _____ be - tray _____ each oth - er.
in - ter - net's _____ gone wild _____ watch - ing mov - ie stars _____ on tri - al while they're

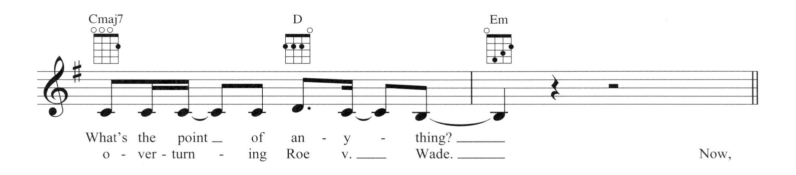

What's the point _____ of an - y - thing? _____
o - ver - turn - ing Roe v. _____ Wade. _____ Now,

Chorus

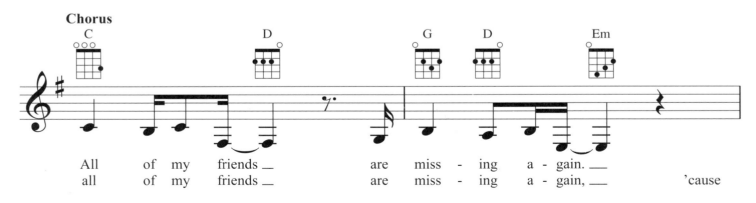

All of my friends _____ are miss - ing a - gain. _____
all of my friends _____ are miss - ing a - gain, _____ 'cause

that's what hap - pens when ___ you fall ___ in love. _____ You
that's what hap - pens when ___ you fall ___ in love. _____ You

don't have the time, ___ you leave them all be - hind. ___ You
don't have the time, ___ you leave them all be - hind. ___ And you

1.
tell your - self ___ it's fine, you're just ___ in love.

2.
love. _____ And I

Bridge

don't get a - long _____ with an - y -

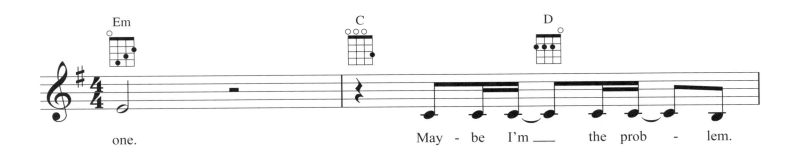

one.   May - be I'm ____ the prob - lem.

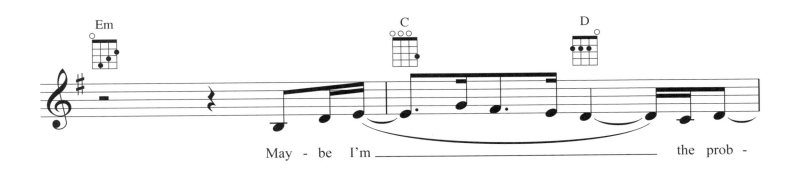

May - be I'm _____ the prob -

Outro 1

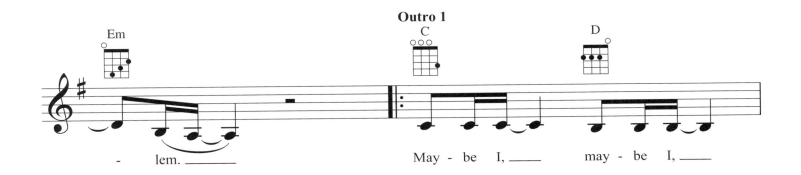

- lem. ____   May - be I, ____   may - be I, ____

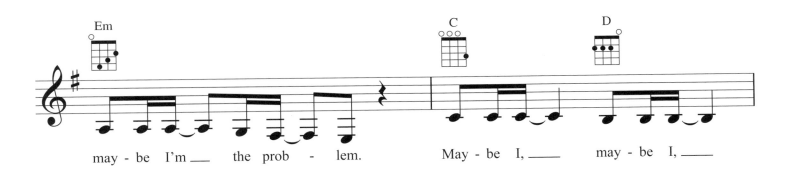

may - be I'm ____ the prob - lem.   May - be I, ____   may - be I, ____

1., 2.   3.

may - be I'm ____ the prob - lem.   may - be I'm ____ the prob - lem.

Outro 2

You Proof

Words and Music by Morgan Wallen, Ashley Gorley, Ryan Vojtesak and Ernest Smith

Copyright © 2022 Bo Wallace Publishing, Big Loud Mountain, Round Hill Songs II, Sony Music Publishing (US) LLC,
Caleb's College Fund, Songs Of Universal, Inc., Big Loud Mountain Music LLC and Ern Dog Music
All Rights for Bo Wallace Publishing and Big Loud Mountain Administered by Round Hill Works
All Rights for Sony Music Publishing (US) LLC and Caleb's College Fund Administered by Sony Music Publishing (US) LLC,
424 Church Street, Suite 1200, Nashville, TN 37219
All Rights for Big Loud Mountain Music LLC and Ern Dog Music Administered by Songs Of Universal, Inc.
All Rights Reserved   Used by Permission

nothing makes you go away. _____ I need something

𝄋 Chorus

you ___ proof, something stronger than I'm

used ___ to. _____ Yeah, I been pulling

ninety to a hundred, feel like nothing's gonna cut it. That's the

hard __ truth. Yeah, I need something you __ proof.

To Coda ⊕

Oh, I need something you _____ proof. _____

Bridge

Poured 'em up till they're shut - ting 'em down, __ yeah.

You nev - er ain't not a - round, __ yeah. Don't mat - ter what time or town,

I can't get you gone. _____ Turned the bar, yeah, up - side down,

just look - ing for some - thing that does it. I'd give 'em all my mon - ey,

D.S. al Coda

ain't no - bod - y sell - ing noth - ing

Coda

Interlude

2. Hey, I been mix - ing

73

74

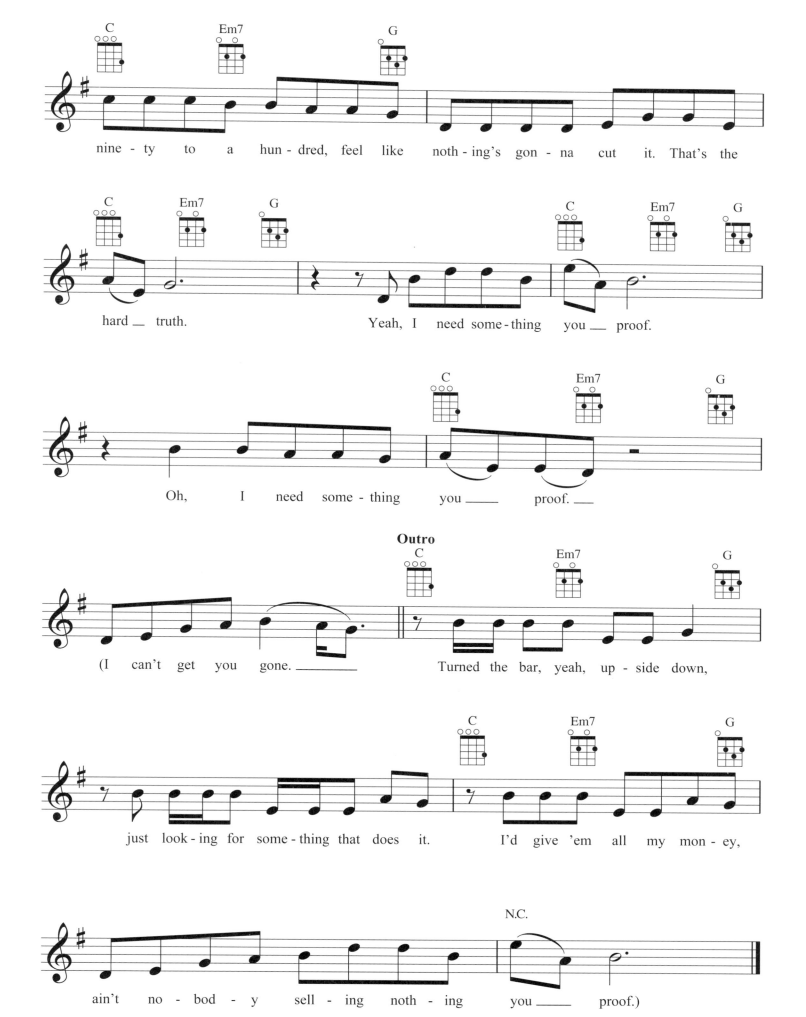

Victoria's Secret

Words and Music by Dan Henig, Mark Nilan Jr. and Jacqueline Miskanic

1. God, I wish some-bod-y would have told me when I was young-er that all bod-ies aren't ___ the same. Pho-to-shop, it-ty bit-ty mod-els on mag-a-zine cov-ers told me I was o-ver-weight. I stopped eat-ing, what a bum-mer. Can't have carbs and a hot girl sum-mer. If I could go back and tell my-self when I was

Copyright © 2022 And The Melody Is, Artist 101 Publishing Group and HelloJax Productions
All Rights for And The Melody Is and Artist 101 Publishing Group Administered Worldwide by Songs Of Kobalt Music Publishing
All Rights Reserved   Used by Permission

to - ri - a _____ was made up by a dude. ___

Verse

_____ 2. I wish some - bod - y would have told me that thighs of

thun - der meant nor - mal hu - man thighs. The fuck - ing pres - sure I was un -

- der to lose my ap - pe - tite and fight the cel - lu - lite with

Hun - ger Games like ev - 'ry night. If I could go back and tell my - self when I was

D.S. al Coda

young - er, I'd say, "Hey, dum - my..."

Coda

to - ri - a _____ was made up by a dude. __

The Best Collections for Ukulele

The Best Songs Ever
70 songs have now been arranged for ukulele. Includes: Always • Bohemian Rhapsody • Memory • My Favorite Things • Over the Rainbow • Piano Man • What a Wonderful World • Yesterday • You Raise Me Up • and more.
00282413 . . . . $17.99

Campfire Songs for Ukulele
30 favorites to sing as you roast marshmallows and strum your uke around the campfire. Includes: God Bless the U.S.A. • Hallelujah • The House of the Rising Sun • I Walk the Line • Puff the Magic Dragon • Wagon Wheel • You Are My Sunshine • and more.
00129170 . . . . . . $15.99

The Daily Ukulele
arr. Liz and Jim Beloff
Strum a different song everyday with easy arrangements of 365 of your favorite songs in one big songbook! Includes favorites by the Beatles, Beach Boys, and Bob Dylan, folk songs, pop songs, kids' songs, Christmas carols, and Broadway and Hollywood tunes, all with a spiral binding for ease of use.
00240356 Original Edition $44.99
00240681 Leap Year Edition $44.99
00119270 Portable Edition $39.99

Disney Hits for Ukulele
Play 23 of your favorite Disney songs on your ukulele. Includes: The Bare Necessities • Cruella De Vil • Do You Want to Build a Snowman? • Kiss the Girl • Lava • Let It Go • Once upon a Dream • A Whole New World • and more.
00151250 . . . . . . $16.99

Also available:
00291547 Disney Fun Songs for Ukulele $17.99
00701708 Disney Songs for Ukulele $15.99
00334696 First 50 Disney Songs on Ukulele $22.99

First 50 Songs You Should Play on Ukulele
An amazing collec-tion of 50 accessible, must-know favorites: Edelweiss • Hey, Soul Sister • I Walk the Line • I'm Yours • Imagine • Over the Rainbow • Peaceful Easy Feeling • The Rainbow Connection • Riptide • more.
00149250 . . . . $19.99
Also available:
00292982 First 50 Melodies on Ukulele $16.99
00289029 First 50 Songs on Solo Ukulele $16.99
00347437 First 50 Songs to Strum on Uke $19.99

40 Most Streamed Songs for Ukulele
40 top hits that sound great on uke! Includes: Despacito • Feel It Still • Girls like You • Happier • Havana • High Hopes • The Middle • Perfect • 7 Rings • Shallow • Shape of You • Something Just like This • Stay • Sucker • Sunflower • Sweet but Psycho • Thank U, Next • There's Nothing Holdin' Me Back • Without Me • and more!
00298113 . . . . $17.99

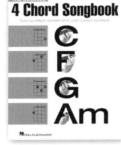

The 4 Chord Songbook
With just 4 chords, you can play 50 hot songs on your ukulele! Songs include: Brown Eyed Girl • Do Wah Diddy Diddy • Hey Ya! • Ho Hey • Jessie's Girl • Let It Be • One Love • Stand by Me • Toes • With or Without You • and many more.
00142050 . . . . $17.99
Also available:
00141143 The 3-Chord Songbook $17.99

Pop Songs for Kids
30 easy pop favorites for kids to play on uke, including: Brave • Can't Stop the Feeling! • Feel It Still • Fight Song • Happy • Havana • House of Gold • How Far I'll Go • Let It Go • Remember Me (Ernesto de la Cruz) • Rewrite the Stars • Roar • Shake It Off • Story of My Life • What Makes You Beautiful • and more.
00284415 . . . . $17.99

Simple Songs for Ukulele
50 favorites for standard G-C-E-A ukulele tuning, including: All Along the Watchtower • Can't Help Falling in Love • Don't Worry, Be Happy • Ho Hey • I'm Yours • King of the Road • Sweet Home Alabama • You Are My Sunshine • and more.
00156815 . . . . $15.99
Also available:
00276644 More Simple Songs for Ukulele $14.99

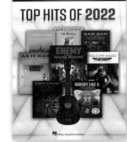

Top Hits of 2022
This collection features 16 of today's top hits arranged with vocal melody, lyrics, and chord diagrams for standard G-C-E-A tuning for ukulele. Songs include: As It Was • Bam Bam • Carolina • Enemy • Freedom • Glimpse of Us • Hold My Hand • Light Switch • Love Me More • Nobody like U • Numb Little Bug • On My Way • Running up That Hill • and more.
01100312 . . . . $14.99
Also available:
00355553 Top Hits of 2020 . . . . $14.99
00302274 Top Hits of 2019 . . . . $14.99

Ukulele: The Most Requested Songs
Strum & Sing Series
Cherry Lane Music
Nearly 50 favorites all expertly arranged for ukulele! Includes: Bubbly • Build Me Up, Buttercup • Cecilia • Georgia on My Mind • Kokomo • L-O-V-E • Your Body Is a Wonderland • and more.
02501453 . . . . $15.99

The Ultimate Ukulele Fake Book
Uke enthusiasts will love this giant, spiral-bound collection of over 400 songs for uke! Includes: Crazy • Dancing Queen • Downtown • Fields of Gold • Happy • Hey Jude • 7 Years • Summertime • Thinking Out Loud • Thriller • Wagon Wheel • and more.
00175500 9" x 12" Edition $45.00
00319997 5.5" x 8.5" Edition $39.99

Order today from your favorite music retailer at
halleonard.com

Prices, contents and availability subject to change without notice

Disney characters and artwork TM & © 2021 Disney

0323
479